Mind Hackers

Decrypting the Enigma of Learning Theory

Freudian Trips

Copyright Page

Disclaimer

The views and opinions expressed in this book are those of the author(s) and do not necessarily reflect the official policy or position of any other agency, organization, employer, or company. The contents of this book are for informational and educational purposes only and are not intended to serve as professional advice, diagnosis, or treatment.

The information provided in this book is believed to be accurate and reliable as of the date of publication. However, it may include some errors or inaccuracies, and no warranty or guarantee is provided regarding the accuracy, timeliness, or applicability of the content.

Readers are encouraged to consult with professional philosophers, educators, or other qualified professionals where appropriate for personalized advice. The author(s) and publisher shall not be liable for any loss, damage, or harm caused or alleged to be caused, directly or indirectly, by the information or ideas contained, suggested, or referenced in this book.

By reading this book, the reader acknowledges and agrees that they are solely responsible for how they interpret and apply the information contained herein.

This book may also include references to other works, studies, and sources. These references are provided for further reading and exploration and do not imply endorsement or validation of the specific theories, viewpoints, or interpretations presented in those works.

Introduction: Ready for the Mind Hack

Ever wondered why some lessons stick like superglue in our brains while others slip away like water through a sieve? Or why some people seem to pick up new languages or instruments effortlessly, while others labor over them for years? If you've asked yourself these questions, congratulations – you're already on the path to understanding the fascinating world of learning theory. And guess what? By the end of this book, not only will you have answers to those questions, but you'll also hold the keys to hacking your own mind for optimal learning.

What's Learning Theory Anyway?

Let's start with a simple analogy. Imagine your brain as a vast, intricate city with roads, pathways, and connections leading everywhere. Now, every time you learn something new, you're essentially building a new pathway or strengthening an existing one in this sprawling city. The "rules" and "strategies" that dictate how these pathways are formed, maintained, and accessed is what we call learning theory. In essence, learning theory is like the rulebook to the game of 'Building the Best Brain City'.

Why Should I Care About How I Learn?

Well, for starters, understanding how we learn can change our lives. It's like finding the cheat codes to a video game. With these codes, or strategies from learning theory, we can:

Speed up our learning process: No more spending hours on topics you just can't seem to grasp!

Enhance memory retention: Forget being forgetful! It's time to remember and recall information more effectively.

Boost motivation and reduce frustration: When you understand the "how" of learning, it becomes a more enjoyable process, with fewer roadblocks and pitfalls.

Achieve personal and professional goals: Whether it's picking up a new hobby or advancing in your career, mastering the art of learning can be your secret weapon.

So, What's in Store for Me in This Book?

Great question! You're about to embark on an exhilarating journey into the mechanics of the mind. Here's a little sneak peek into our itinerary:

We'll revisit the legends who laid the foundations of learning theory. Think of them as the original architects of 'Brain City'.

Discover how learning has evolved in the age of digital wonders. Screens, apps, games – how do they reshape the way we learn?

Dive deep into strategies and hacks to fine-tune your own learning. Tailored for everyone, whether you're a student, a professional, or someone just curious about the brain's marvels.

Confront myths, misconceptions, and the tricky pitfalls in the world of learning. We'll debunk myths and arm you with tools to navigate the modern information overload.

Finally, let's dream and speculate about the future of learning. With technology advancing at warp speed, how will our learning adapt and transform?

Ready to Jump In?

Remember, every master was once a beginner. Every expert started with the basics. And every mind – yes, including yours – has untapped potential. So, buckle up, because we're about to embark on a journey to unlock that potential.

In this guide, there's no jargon, no complicated terminology, just simple, engaging, and actionable insights. Ready for the mind hack? Let's go!

Chapter 1: Decoding Learning - Your Guide to Understanding This Powerful Process

Ever felt like your brain is a giant puzzle? And you don't have the box with the picture to figure out how all the pieces fit together? Well, this chapter will give you that box! We're going to decode the mystery of learning by creating a simple yet comprehensive roadmap to this fascinating process.

Let's start with the basics. What is learning anyway? Simply put, it's the act of acquiring new knowledge or skills. Seems simple enough, but here's the important part - it actually takes many different forms. Shall we explore some of the most common types together?

Observational learning is when we learn just by watching others. Mmm hmm, like a baby learning to clap by looking at the happy adults around them. The technical term for this is modeling, but let's keep it simple. See someone do something awesome? Your brain can soak that up through observation alone!

Motor learning is mastering physical movements and tasks through repetition and practice. Remember learning to ride a bike or play the guitar? Those new skills didn't develop overnight; it took practice to train your muscles and nerves to work together. That's motor learning in a nutshell.

With relational learning, you make connections between bits of information and tie them together in your mind. This type helps you draw conclusions, infer things, and solve problems by relating new stuff to existing knowledge. How neat is that?

And let's not forget spatial learning - understanding spaces, navigating environments, and creating mental maps. Think of all the times you've learned to get around a new place. Your handy mental GPS is thanks to spatial learning!

Now that we've unlocked some secrets of different learning types, let's move on to the impact of this knowledge. You see, understanding learning isn't just useful for students to ace tests. It also benefits teachers, psychologists, doctors and more!

For teachers, learning theory helps create lessons that sync up with how we learn best. For psychologists, it provides insight into human behavior and development. For medical experts, it shows how the brain changes physically as we learn. See, fascinating stuff!

Alright, we've covered a lot of ground in this intro chapter. So give yourself a pat on the back! Together, we've started decoding the powerful process of learning. With this foundation, we can continue our discovery by digging deeper in the upcoming chapters. Let's keep exploring - your guide is right here with you every step of the way!

Chapter 2: The Original Mind Hackers: Classic Learning Theorists

Imagine a time when the human mind was a vast, mysterious frontier, waiting to be explored. Just as adventurers once sought out new lands, there were daring thinkers who delved into the realm of the brain and how we learn. They're our "Original Mind Hackers", and their discoveries laid the foundation for everything we understand about learning today. Let's meet them!

1. Pavlov and His Drooling Dogs

Imagine you're in a kitchen. The delightful smell of freshly baked cookies fills the air. What's your first reaction? If you thought, "I'm hungry," you're not alone! Now, every time you smell cookies, you might think of eating. But why?

A scientist named Ivan Pavlov had a similar question. Dogs would begin to drool when they saw the person who usually fed them as well as when they saw food, he observed. Pavlov rang a bell each time he fed the dogs in order to investigate this. After a while, even when there was no food nearby, the dogs started to slobber at the sound of the bell! This is known as Classical Conditioning. Basically, our brains can associate two unrelated things if they're presented together often enough. Like associating the smell of cookies with hunger.

2. Skinner's Bird Box Adventures

Ever tried teaching a pet a new trick and rewarded them with a treat when they did it right? You can thank B.F. Skinner for that technique!

Skinner placed hungry birds in a box with a button. When the bird accidentally pressed the button, out came food. Soon, the birds learned to press the button on purpose to get the treat. This is called Operant Conditioning. It's all about rewards and consequences. If an action leads to a reward (like food for the bird), we're more likely to do it again. If it leads to something not-so-nice, we'll probably avoid doing it in the future.

3. Bandura's Monkey See, Monkey Do

Have you ever tried mimicking someone's dance moves or copied a friend's style? It's not just because you admired them; it's a fundamental way we learn!

Albert Bandura showed that we can learn just by observing others. He famously demonstrated this with an experiment where children watched an adult play aggressively with a toy. Later on, those children played aggressively with the toy too, mimicking what they had observed. This is known as Social Learning Theory. Simply put, we don't just learn by doing; we also learn by watching!

4. Piaget's Puzzling Playtime

When children play, it's not just fun and games. To Jean Piaget, playtime was a window into how children think and learn.

Piaget believed that as we grow, our understanding of the world shifts through different stages. For example, young children might think the moon follows them because it seems to move as they walk. As they get older and learn more, their view changes. This is the essence of Cognitive Learning Theory. Our understanding of the world evolves as we gather more information and experiences.

Our Original Mind Hackers were pioneers, making groundbreaking discoveries with each experiment. From drooling dogs to button-pushing birds, from mimicking moves to playful puzzles, these theorists unveiled the rich tapestry of how we learn. They showed us that learning is a dance between our environment, our experiences, and our ever-evolving minds.

Stay curious, dear reader. Just as these thinkers unlocked the mysteries of their time, who knows what you might discover with the tools of understanding they've passed down to us?

Chapter 3: The Learner Awakens - Embracing Active Learning

Learning. For a long time, the common approach treated it like a passive process. Just sit there and absorb whatever the teacher says, right? Wrong! This chapter will explain the paradigm shift to active learning and why it's so important. Read on to awaken your inner learner!

First, let's examine this change in detail. Traditional education methods focused on passive learning. Students quietly listened to lectures, memorized facts, and regurgitated info. Boring!

Fortunately, new theories recognize that effective learning requires more involvement from the learner. Active participation, hands-on practice, two-way discussions - that's how we truly learn and remember!

Cognitive and constructivist theories paved the way for this change. They emphasize that students construct their own knowledge. Learners are seen as active participants rather than just empty vessels waiting to be filled. Makes sense!

Active learning engages you directly in the process. You discuss, experiment, solve problems, work on projects, and apply concepts. No more just sitting there zoning out! You take an active role in your own learning.

This shift is vital. Passive learning is limiting. Without involvement, our motivation suffers and we fail to develop higher-order thinking skills. Active learning keeps us alert, energized, and invested in the experience.

So embrace the power you have as an active learner! Question ideas, make connections to your life, discuss topics with others. Stay curious. This active mindset will open you up to deeper learning.

The change is here. The learner awakening is underway. Are you ready to take charge of your learning journey? Your active participation is the key that unlocks your mind's potential. It's an exciting time - let's all be awake and alert as empowered active learners!

Chapter 4: Neuromancy: The Neuroscience of Learning

Imagine if our brains were like cities. There would be busy highways of thoughts, quiet corners of memories, and lively marketplaces of emotions. Now, what if we could peek behind the city's walls and understand the magic that powers it? Welcome to the enchanting world of neuroscience, where we unravel the secrets of our brain's magic!

The Grand Orchestra of the Brain

If you've ever watched an orchestra perform, you'd have seen multiple instruments, each playing its part, coming together to create a beautiful melody. Our brains are like that orchestra. Each tiny part, called a neuron, plays its note, and together they create the song of our thoughts, memories, and emotions.

The Magic of Neural Plasticity

Remember building with blocks or playdough as a kid? You could mold them, reshape them, and even if you squished them flat, you could build them up again. Our brain is a lot like that – always changing, adapting, and reshaping.

This ability of the brain to change is called neural plasticity. It means that every time we learn something new or have a new experience, our brain's structure can change a bit. It's like adding a new road or building to our brain city.

For example, if you learn to play the guitar, certain parts of your brain will get more robust, like exercising a muscle. The more you practice, the stronger these 'guitar-playing' parts become!

Storing Souvenirs: Memory Consolidation

Think of your favorite holiday or a memorable day. Now, isn't it amazing that even after years, you can recall those memories? That's the work of a process called memory consolidation.

Every experience is like buying a souvenir on a trip. Initially, it's just lying around in your bag (short-term memory). But later, you keep it safe in a special cabinet at home (long-term memory). Our brain does something similar. When we sleep or even daydream, it's like our brain is sorting and keeping those souvenirs safe, ensuring we remember them for a long time.

A Treat for Your Thoughts: The Brain's Reward System

Ever wondered why you feel so good when you solve a tricky puzzle or finally understand a challenging concept? It's like the brain's way of giving you a gold star or a sweet treat!

When we achieve something or find something pleasurable, a chemical called dopamine is released in our brain. It's like our brain's candy, making us feel good. This is a part of our brain's reward system. So, when we're learning, and something 'clicks', our brain rewards us with this feel-good sensation. That's why when we're curious and eager, learning becomes more fun and enjoyable.

Embarking on the Brain's Mystical Journey

Neuroscience, or the study of the brain, is like peeling back the layers of a grand, mystical onion. With each layer, we discover more about ourselves, how we think, how we feel, and how we learn. And just like magic, the more we understand, the more enchanted we become.

So, the next time you're learning something new or reminiscing about an old memory, take a moment to marvel at the wonder that is your brain – the grand conductor of the symphony of you.

Chapter 5: The Constructivist Uprising - Building Knowledge Through Experience

Learning isn't just about memorizing facts. It's about constructing knowledge from the building blocks of your own experiences. This chapter explores the constructivist revolution in detail. Read on to learn how you can empower yourself as a hands-on, engaged learner!

Constructivist theories focus on knowledge creation. According to this view, we build learning by integrating new information with our prior knowledge and experiences. Makes sense, right?

For true learning to occur, you need those mental hooks to hang new concepts on. Your own reflections and perceptions shape the knowledge you construct. It's learning by doing, not by passive absorption.

See, you already come equipped with an amazing framework thanks to your background. Constructivists realize honoring your individual experiences is key. You're not just a blank slate!

Plus, social interaction adds important layers to this process. Dialogue, teamwork, and collaborations with others enrich learning.

Think about how you build new understandings by discussing ideas with classmates or coworkers.

Constructivist learning is active and empowering. You take charge of making meanings, not just receiving them. Questions, experiments, creativity - that's how you really learn.

So embrace your experiences! Value your identity, background, and perceptions. Build on your existing knowledge. Discuss ideas socially. This constructivist approach will electrify your learning ability.

The revolution is here! Be an active creator, not a passive receiver. Your constructivist uprising starts now. Let's build some knowledge together.

Chapter 6: The Pedagogical Innovators: Modern Learning Theories

Imagine stepping into a classroom of the future. No more rows of desks facing a chalkboard. Instead, there's the buzz of excitement, students deeply engrossed in projects, discussions, experiments, and multimedia screens showcasing various lessons. Welcome to the world of modern learning – a space where the old-school meets the new-age, all with one mission: making learning an adventure.

1. Inquiry-based Learning: The Curious Explorer's Tool

Do you remember being a kid and asking 'why' about just about everything? "Why is the sky blue? Why do birds fly?" Inquiry-based learning is like giving wings to that curious child in all of us.

Instead of just listening to answers, students are encouraged to ask questions, dive deep, and discover answers for themselves. It's like turning every lesson into a thrilling treasure hunt, where the treasure is knowledge.

2. Project-based Learning: Crafting Knowledge

Think of your favorite DIY or craft project. Remember the joy of creating something from scratch? Project-based learning (PBL) brings that same joy to the classroom.

In PBL, students work on a project over an extended period, say, building a model ecosystem or writing and staging a play. Through this, they don't just learn about a topic; they live it. It's learning by doing, making every lesson a hands-on adventure.

3. Problem-based Learning: The Puzzle Masters

Ever faced a tricky problem and felt the thrill of solving it? Problem-based learning (PBL) is all about that thrill.

Here, students are given real-world problems to solve. For example, "How can we provide clean water to a remote village?" To find solutions, they'd dive into various subjects, collaborate, and think critically. It's not just about finding the right answer but enjoying the journey of getting there.

4. Flipped Classroom: Homework Goes Hollywood

Imagine if homework was watching a cool video, and class time was all about discussions and hands-on activities. Sounds fun, right? That's the flipped classroom for you.

Instead of lectures in class and practice at home, the 'script' is flipped. Students watch videos or read materials at home, and in school, they dive deep into discussions, ask questions, and collaborate on projects. It's like turning the traditional classroom upside-down for more engaging and active learning.

5. Blended Learning: Best of Both Worlds

Imagine a smoothie, where you blend your favorite fruits to get a delicious mix. Blended learning is the educational version of that smoothie.

It mixes traditional classroom teaching with online learning. This way, students can learn at their pace, use multimedia resources, and still have face-to-face interactions with teachers and peers. It's a perfect blend of old and new, giving learners the flexibility and richness they need in today's world.

Shaping the Future, One Theory at a Time

These modern approaches are like a breath of fresh air in the world of learning. They recognize that every learner is unique, every brain a universe of its own, and every lesson a potential adventure.

The beauty of these methods lies in their adaptability. They can be molded to fit different subjects, age groups, and even individual learning styles. It's like having a toolbox, and depending on the task at hand, you pick the tool that suits best.

So, whether you're a student, a teacher, a parent, or just someone eager to learn, remember: the world of modern learning is vast, vibrant, and waiting for you to dive in. Let's turn every lesson into an exploration, every classroom into an innovation hub, and every student into an enthusiastic learner. Welcome to the future of learning!

Chapter 7: The Virtual Odyssey - Learning in the Digital Age

Learning has gone digital! With smartphones, apps, online courses and more, the virtual world is reshaping education. How do classic learning theories apply now? Let's embark on an exciting odyssey together to explore learning in the digital age!

Today's tech opens up new possibilities. Multimedia content engages us across learning styles. Mobile devices make learning accessible anywhere. Web tools connect us with global classrooms. Powerful stuff!

Terms like **e-learning (electronic), m-learning (mobile) and u-learning (ubiquitous)** point to the new opportunities. Online courses allow self-paced learning on your schedule. Knowledge is now only a click away!

Digital education also enables customization. Adaptive learning platforms tailor content based on your strengths and weaknesses. Personalized learning that fits your needs and interests takes center stage.

Gaming elements further enhance the experience. Points, badges, leaderboards - gamification makes learning fun! Who said learning can't feel like playing?

But it's not all unicorn rainbows. Potential distractions loom large. Staring at screens excessively can strain our eyes and minds. We need balance and boundaries.

Still, used wisely, technology can elevate learning. Combining digital engagement with real-world interactions might just be the winning formula.

Our virtual odyssey has shown that learning principles endure, even if the tools evolve. As we boldly venture forth, new frontiers will surely emerge. But knowledge will remain the treasure we all seek.

Onward fellow learners - our journey continues! Digital or analog, the important thing is we never stop learning together.

Chapter 8: The Info-Virus: Misinformation and Cognitive Biases

Picture this: you're browsing the digital realms of the internet when suddenly, an enticing headline catches your eye. It shares an unbelievable fact or a shocking revelation. Without a second thought, you share it with your friends. But later, you discover that what you shared wasn't accurate at all. Oops!

Welcome to the era of the "Info-Virus", where misinformation spreads quickly, and our brains can sometimes trick us into believing things without checking. Let's dive deep into this realm and discover how we can become smarter and more discerning learners.

Misinformation: The Sneaky Impostor

Just like in the game where players find out who the impostor is, in the digital age, it's crucial to figure out which information is genuine and which is pretending to be something it's not. Misinformation is like that sneaky impostor – it looks real, but it's not.

Misinformation can distort our view of the world, affect our decisions, and even shape our beliefs. When we learn something that's not accurate, unlearning it can be a challenge. It's like trying to remove a stubborn stain – the longer it stays, the harder it gets to clear.

Cognitive Biases: The Brain's Shortcuts (and Slip-ups)

Our brains are marvelous, but sometimes they take shortcuts. These shortcuts, known as cognitive biases, are like pre-programmed reactions based on our past experiences, beliefs, or emotions. While they can help us make quick decisions, they can also lead us astray.

For instance, if we hear something from multiple sources (even if they're not credible), we might believe it's true just because many people are talking about it. Or, if information aligns with our beliefs, we're more likely to accept it without questioning. These biases can sometimes make our learning journey resemble a rollercoaster with unexpected twists and turns.

Building Your Info-Immunity: Countering the Viral Spread

So, how do we protect ourselves from the rapid spread of misinformation and the tricks our brains might play on us? Here are some strategies:

Question Everything: Adopt a curious mindset. When you encounter new information, ask: Where did it come from? Is the source trustworthy? Are there other sources that confirm it?

Slow Down: Before hitting that 'share' button or believing something right away, take a moment to pause. Double-check facts, especially if they elicit strong emotions.

Educate Yourself About Biases: Knowing is half the battle. Once you're aware of common biases, you'll be better equipped to notice when they might be affecting your thinking.

Engage in Open Conversations: Talk to people with different viewpoints. It can help you see things from multiple perspectives and break free from the echo chambers that often reinforce our existing beliefs.

Cultivate a Growth Mindset: Accept that you might be wrong sometimes. Being open to changing your mind based on new evidence is a sign of growth and learning.

Navigating the Digital Maze

In the age of information overload, being a discerning learner is both a challenge and a necessity. By understanding the pitfalls of misinformation and biases and equipping ourselves with the right tools, we can navigate the vast digital maze with confidence.

Remember, it's not about knowing everything but rather about being discerning, curious, and open to growth. Equip yourself, be vigilant, and happy learning!

Chapter 9: The Master Key - Unlocking Learning Theories in the Real World

Theories and concepts are great, but what about real-world application? This chapter will provide the master key to unlock learning theories where it matters - in classrooms, workplaces, and your daily life!

Let's start with examples. Ms. Jackson revamped her lesson plans to align with active learning theories. Now students participate in lively discussions and hands-on activities. The results? Higher engagement and test scores!

At A+ Software Inc., employees learn programming best practices through on-the-job training. Daniel shadowed Angela while she coded new features. Collaborative learning in action!

Even in everyday situations, we can apply learning insights. Nick struggled with memorizing Spanish vocabulary. So he made flash-cards with visuals - great use of multi-modal learning!

What other winning strategies can learning theories offer? Here are a few to consider:

Use repetition and mnemonics to boost memorization

Seek diverse perspectives when problem-solving

Connect new knowledge to your experiences

Test yourself frequently to reinforce learning

The key is choosing approaches that work for your learning style and needs. With so many theories out there, find what clicks for you!

Learning mastery is within reach. With the right strategies, you can unlock your potential in any environment. This chapter aimed to bridge theory with practical tools. Go forth and keep learning, in classrooms and beyond!

Chapter 10: Beyond the Frontier: Future Trends in Learning Theory

Imagine boarding a spaceship, destined to explore the vast expanse of the universe. Each star and planet represents a unique way of learning, a different theory, a new approach. We're about to embark on a journey beyond the known, peering into what the future might hold for the way we learn.

Current Constellations: Today's Research Highlights

Before we launch into the uncharted territories, let's glance at the bright stars currently lighting up the field of learning theory.

Personalized Learning: Much like streaming services suggest movies based on our preferences, modern learning tools are tailoring educational experiences according to individual learners' needs.

Virtual and Augmented Reality: By donning a headset, students can now walk through ancient ruins or dissect virtual frogs, making learning more immersive.

Emotional Intelligence in Learning: Recognizing and addressing emotions can dramatically affect learning outcomes. Today's researchers are keen on integrating emotional health with educational approaches.

The Horizon Ahead: Predictions and Prophecies

With the pace of technology and societal change, predicting the future can feel like gazing into a crystal ball. But based on current trajectories, here are some educated guesses:

Neuro-Enhanced Learning: As our understanding of the brain deepens, future learning might involve techniques directly stimulating specific brain areas to enhance memory or cognition.

AI-Powered Mentors: Imagine a digital companion that knows your learning style, habits, strengths, and areas of growth. This AI entity could guide, mentor, and offer personalized resources throughout one's learning journey.

Learning through Simulation: We might soon have intricate simulations where learners can play out various scenarios – from running a business to solving global crises – and learn from virtual experiences.

Implications and Inspirations: The Brave New World

The future, while exciting, also brings forth a realm of questions and considerations:

Ethical Boundaries: As we integrate more technology, where do we draw the line? Neuro-enhancements, for instance, could raise concerns about authenticity and equity in learning.

Human Touch in AI Era: With AI playing a pivotal role, how do we ensure that the human touch, the personal connections that enrich the learning process, isn't lost?

Accessibility: As we advance, it's crucial to ensure that these innovative learning tools and techniques are accessible to all, irrespective of their socio-economic backgrounds.

Setting Sail into the Cosmos of Learning

As we stand on the brink of these exciting frontiers, one thing remains clear: the landscape of learning is ever-evolving. With each new discovery, methodology, or tool, we inch closer to understanding the vast universe of the human mind and how best it grasps knowledge.

So, as you continue your journey, whether as a teacher, student, or lifelong learner, remember to gaze often at the stars, stay curious, and be open to the limitless possibilities that the future of learning promises.

The universe of knowledge awaits. Are you ready to explore?

Conclusion: From Theory to Mastery - Your Journey to Lifelong Learning

We've reached the final stop on our journey together through the fascinating world of learning theories. Let's recap the main takeaways before we part ways:

Many types of learning exist, from observational to relational to motor and more. Understanding these modalities is key to decoding how we acquire knowledge.

Active learning promotes deeper engagement than passive approaches. Empower yourself as a motivated participant in the learning process!

Constructivist methods that leverage prior experience and social interaction can boost learning. Build on your existing foundations.

Technology opens new doors, but also requires balance. Use digital tools wisely to enhance real-world learning.

Most importantly, keep applying theories in everyday practice. Let these insights guide you as a lifelong learner!

Learning is a treasure that never loses its shine. Whether in classrooms or careers, relationships or hobbies, there are always new frontiers to explore. I hope this book sparked an enduring curiosity within you.

Your journey continues well beyond these pages. I encourage you to take these theories and make them your own. Experiment, refine your approach, and share your discoveries with others.

It has been my sincerest pleasure to navigate this terrain together. May your days ahead overflow with the joys of lifelong learning! Always keep growing. The best is yet to come.

Farewell for now, fellow traveler! Your next exciting destination awaits...

Appendix: Mind Hackers' Toolbox

Welcome to the Mind Hackers' Toolbox! Consider this your handy-dandy guide to some key terms we've covered throughout our journey. We've carefully crafted simple and easy-to-understand definitions, ensuring that everyone, from beginners to seasoned learners, can grasp the concepts. Let's dive in!

Glossary of Key Terms

Personalized Learning: Tailoring education to fit the unique needs and preferences of each learner. Imagine if a teacher could give every student a unique lesson plan that matches their pace and style. That's the essence of personalized learning!

Virtual Reality (VR): A computer-generated environment that you can explore and interact with. It's like stepping into a video game or a movie, where you are part of the action.

Augmented Reality (AR): Overlaying computer-generated images or information onto the real world. It's like if you could see digital information (like game characters or directions) on top of what you normally see.

Emotional Intelligence: Understanding, using, and managing our emotions in positive ways. It's about recognizing our feelings and those of others, and using this knowledge to guide our actions.

Neuro-Enhanced Learning: Techniques or tools that directly interact with the brain to boost memory or understanding. Think of it as giving the brain a little "boost" to help it learn better.

AI-Powered Mentors: Digital helpers or guides, powered by Artificial Intelligence, that can understand your learning habits and give you personalized advice. It's like having a smart robot tutor who knows just how you like to learn.

Simulation: A model or imitation of a situation. It allows learners to practice or experience something in a controlled environment. Imagine practicing how to fly a plane on the computer before doing it for real!

Cognitive Biases: These are like the brain's "shortcuts" which can sometimes lead us to incorrect conclusions. For example, if you've always had amazing chocolate cake on birthdays, you might quickly assume that all chocolate cakes (even ones you haven't tasted) are amazing.

Misinformation: Wrong or inaccurate information that is spread, whether intentionally or not. It's like hearing a rumor that's not true but believing and sharing it because it sounds convincing.

Blended Learning: A mix of traditional classroom teaching and online education. Think of it as a class where you learn in person and through digital resources, combining the best of both worlds.

Flipped Classroom: A teaching method where traditional learning is turned on its head. Students first study the topic by themselves, typically using video lessons, and then apply what they've learned in class with the teacher's guidance.

And that wraps up our toolbox! Remember, the journey of learning is continuous. As you move ahead, armed with this newfound knowledge, may you find joy in every discovery and curiosity in every challenge. The universe of learning is vast, and you're well-equipped to explore its wonders. Happy hacking!

About Freudian Trips

Welcome to Freudian Trips, your dedicated platform for diving deep into the world of psychology. We are more than just a YouTube channel or a book publisher. We are a beacon of enlightenment, making complex psychological concepts accessible and engaging for all.

Our YouTube channel is a rich repository of psychology made simple. We take the profound and often complex ideas from the world of psychology and break them down into digestible, easy-to-understand content. From the foundational theories of Freud to the cognitive insights of Piaget, we cover a broad spectrum of psychological schools and thoughts, making psychology accessible to everyone, regardless of their background or prior knowledge.

As a book publisher, we take the same approach, transforming intricate psychological theories into comprehensible narratives. Our books are not just collections of words, but vessels of wisdom that make psychology approachable and relatable. We believe that psychology should not be confined to academic circles, but should be available to all who seek to understand the human mind and behavior.

At Freudian Trips, we believe in the power of curiosity and the pursuit of knowledge. We are here to stoke the fires of your curiosity, to guide you on your intellectual journey, and to help you navigate the fascinating world of psychology.

If you are someone who is not afraid to question, to explore, and to learn, then you are in the right place. Join us on this journey of exploration, as we make psychology easy to understand, one concept at a time.

Be sure to visit our Youtube channel at: www.freudiantrips.com/youtube

You can also visit us on the web at www.freudiantrips.com

Welcome to The Freudian Trip community. Stay curious. Stay enlightened.